Walking with God in Every Season

KAY ARTHUR
PETE De LACY

HARVEST HOUSE PUBLISHERS
EUGENE, OREGON

Cover by Koechel Peterson & Associates, Inc., Minneapolis, Minnesota

WALKING WITH GOD IN EVERY SEASON
Copyright © 2010 by Precept Ministries International
Published by Harvest House Publishers
Eugene, Oregon 97402
www.harvesthousepublishers.com

Library of Congress Cataloging-in-Publication Data

Arthur, Kay
  Walking with God in every season / Kay Arthur and Pete De Lacy.
   p. cm.
  ISBN 978-0-7369-2236-4 (pbk.)
  1. Bible. O.T. Ecclesiastes—Criticism, interpretation, etc   2. Bible. O.T. Song of Solomon—Criticism, interpretation, etc.   3. Bible. O.T. Lamentations—Criticism, interpretation, etc.
  I. De Lacy, Pete. II. Title.
  BS1475.55.A78 2010
  223.'06—dc22

                                                    2009025870

Printed in the United States of America

10 11 12 13 14 15 16 / BP-NI / 10 9 8 7 6 5 4 3 2 1

CONTENTS

How to Get Started...

ᘓᕪᘓᕪ

Reading directions is sometimes difficult and hardly ever enjoyable! Most often you just want to get started. Only if all else fails will you read the instructions. We understand, but please don't approach this study that way. These brief instructions are a vital part of getting started on the right foot and will help you immensely.

FIRST

As you study Ecclesiastes, Song of Solomon, and Lamentations, you will need four things in addition to this book:

1. A Bible you are willing to mark in. The marking is essential. An ideal Bible for this purpose is *The New Inductive Study Bible (NISB)*. The *NISB* is in a single-column text format with large, easy-to-read type, which is ideal for marking. The margins of the text are wide and blank so you can take notes.

The *NISB* also has instructions for studying each book of the Bible, but it does not contain any commentary on the text, nor is it compiled from any theological stance. Its purpose is to teach you how to discern truth for yourself through the inductive method of study. (The three charts you will find in this study guide are taken from the *NISB*.)

Whichever Bible you use, just know you will need to mark in it, which brings us to the second item you will need…

2. A fine-point, four-color ballpoint pen or various colored fine-point pens that you can use to write in your Bible. Office supply stores should have these.

3. Colored pencils or an eight-color leaded Pentel pencil.

4. A composition book or a notebook for working on your assignments and recording your insights.

SECOND

1. As you study Ecclesiastes, Song of Solomon, and Lamentations, you will be given specific instructions for each day's study. These should take you between 20 and 30 minutes a day, but if you spend more time than this, you will increase your intimacy with the Word of God and the God of the Word.

If you are doing this study in a class and you find the lessons too heavy, simply do what you can. To do a little is better than to do nothing. Don't be an all-or-nothing person when it comes to Bible study.

Remember, anytime you get into the Word of God, you enter into more intensive warfare with the devil (our enemy). Why? Every piece of the Christian's armor is related to the Word of God. And our one and only offensive weapon is the sword of the Spirit, which is the Word of God. The enemy wants you to have a dull sword. Don't cooperate! You don't have to!

2. As you read each passage from the Bible, train yourself to ask the "5 W's and an H": who, what, when, where, why, and how. Asking questions like these helps you see exactly what the Word of God is saying. When you interrogate the text with the 5 W's and an H, you ask questions like these:

What is the chapter about?

Who are the main characters?

When does this event or teaching take place?

Where does this happen?

Why is this being done or said?

How did it happen?

3. Locations are important in many books of the Bible, so marking references to these in a distinguishable way will be helpful to you. We simply underline every reference to a location in green (grass and trees are green!) using a four-color ballpoint pen.

4. References to time are also very important and should be marked in an easily recognizable way in your Bible. We mark them by putting a clock like this 🕐 in the margin of the Bible beside the verse where the phrase occurs. You may want to underline or color the references to time in one specific color.

5. You will be given certain key words to mark throughout this study. This is the purpose of the colored pencils and the colored pens. If you will develop the habit of marking your Bible in this way, you will find it will make a significant difference in the effectiveness of your study and in how much you remember.

A key word is an important word that the author uses repeatedly in order to convey his message to his readers. Certain key words will show up throughout an entire book; others will be concentrated in specific chapters. When you mark a key word, you should also mark its synonyms (words that mean the same thing in the context) and any pronouns (*I, me, my, mine; you, your, yours; he, him, his; she, her, hers; it, its; we, us, our, ours; they, them, their, theirs...*) in the same way you marked the key word. Also, mark each word the same way in all of its forms (such as *judge, judgment,* and *judging*). We will give you a few suggestions for ways to mark key words in your daily assignments.

You can use colors or symbols or a combination of colors and symbols to mark words for easy identification. However, colors are easier to distinguish than symbols. When we use symbols, we keep them very simple. For example, you could draw a red heart around the word *love* and shade the inside of the heart like this: love.

When we mark the members of the Godhead (which we do not always do), we color each word yellow and mark *Father* with a purple triangle like this: Father. We mark *Son* this way: Son, and *Holy Spirit* this way: Spirit.

Mark key words in a way that is easy for you to remember.

Devising a color-coding system for marking key words throughout your Bible will help you instantly see where a key word is used. To keep track of your key words, list them on a three-by-five card and mark them the way you mark them in your Bible. You can use this card as a bookmark.

6. An AT A GLANCE chart is included at the end of each section of this book. As you complete your study of a chapter, record the main theme of that chapter under the appropriate chapter number. The main theme of a chapter is what the chapter deals with the most. It may be a particular subject or teaching.

If you will fill out the AT A GLANCE charts as you progress through the study, you will have a synopsis of each book when you are finished. If you have a copy of *The New Inductive Study Bible,* you will find the same charts on pages 1077, 1088, and 1315. If you record your themes there, you will have them for a ready reference.

7. Always begin your study with prayer. As you do your part to handle the Word of God accurately, you must remember that the Bible is a divinely inspired book. The words that you are reading are truth, given to you by God so you can know Him and His ways more intimately. These truths are divinely revealed.

> For to us God revealed them through the Spirit;
> for the Spirit searches all things, even the depths of
> God. For who among men knows the thoughts of
> a man except the spirit of the man which is in him?
> Even so the thoughts of God no one knows except
> the Spirit of God (1 Corinthians 2:10-11).

Therefore ask God to reveal His truth to you as He leads and guides you into all truth. He will if you will ask.

8. Each day when you finish your lesson, meditate on what you saw. Ask your heavenly Father how you should live in light of the truths you have just studied. At times, depending on how God has spoken to you through His Word, you might even want to write LFL ("Lessons for Life") in the margin of your Bible and then, as briefly as possible, record the lesson for life that you want to remember.

THIRD

This study is set up so that you have an assignment for every day of the week—so that you are in the Word daily. If you work through your study in this way, you will benefit more than if you do a week's study in one sitting. Pacing yourself this way allows time for thinking through what you learn on a daily basis!

The seventh day of each week differs from the other six days. The seventh day is designed to aid group discussion. However, it's also profitable if you are studying this book individually.

The "seventh" day is whatever day in the week you choose to finish your week's study. On this day, you will find a verse or two for you to memorize and STORE IN YOUR HEART. Then there is a passage to READ AND DISCUSS. This will help you focus on a major truth or major truths covered in your study that week.

We have included QUESTIONS FOR DISCUSSION OR INDIVIDUAL STUDY to assist those using this book in a Sunday school class or a group Bible study. Taking the time to answer these questions will help you apply the truth to your own life even if you are not doing this study with anyone else.

If you are in a group, be sure every member of the class, including the teacher, supports his or her answers and insights from the Bible text itself. Then you will be handling the Word of God accurately. As you learn to see what the text says and compare Scripture with Scripture, the Bible explains itself.

Always examine your insights by carefully observing the text to see what it *says*. Then, before you decide what the passage of Scripture *means*, make sure that you interpret it in the light of its context. Scripture will never contradict Scripture. If it ever seems to contradict the rest of the Word of God, you can be certain that something is being taken out of context. If you come to a passage that is difficult to understand, reserve your interpretations for a time when you can study the passage in greater depth.

The purpose of the Thought for the Week is to share with you what we consider to be an important element in your week of study. We have included it for your evaluation and, we hope, for your edification. This section will help you see how to walk in light of what you learned.

Books in the New Inductive Study Series are survey courses. If you want to do a more in-depth study of a particular book of the Bible, we suggest you do a Precept Upon Precept Bible study course on that book. You may obtain more information on these courses by contacting Precept Ministries International at 800-763-8280, visiting our website at www.precept.org, or filling out and mailing the response card in the back of this book.

ECCLESIASTES

INTRODUCTION
TO ECCLESIASTES

Solomon, the son of David and king of Israel, was the wisest man the world had ever seen. Yet he wondered about the meaning of life. He wondered about the things man can achieve and their value in life and in death.

Perhaps you too have thought of these things, of life's ups and downs, wondering about them and searching your heart and mind to understand what life is all about. As you study Ecclesiastes, you'll find new meaning in this search, and you'll gain new understanding as well. The purpose of Ecclesiastes, Song of Solomon, and Lamentations is to lead you into a knowledge of the truth.

The key to understanding life better is knowing God, which of course is more than simply knowing about God. If we don't know God, we can't understand His character or ways. God is the source of life, so knowing His character and ways sheds light on our lives. That's how we learn what's important (His purposes for our life) and what's not (the things we plan apart from Him).

Ecclesiastes records Solomon's investigation into the meaning of life, his search to understand what man's life is about and how people can know God. Sometimes it's difficult to put ourselves in the place of someone who lived 3000 years ago. It's hard to shed our present circumstances and think of life without the revelation we have received in the Lord Jesus Christ. But as we study Ecclesiastes, we discover what Solomon knew about God—what God had revealed about Himself from the time of Adam up to Solomon's day. And by comparing Scripture with Scripture, we discover even more because God continued to reveal Himself after Solomon's time.

Because God reveals Himself today through His Word, we'll learn about God for ourselves. And we'll learn what's best for us—how we can apply God's truth and wisdom to our lives.

THERE IS NOTHING NEW
UNDER THE SUN

∾∾∾∾

The sun rises, the sun sets. Nothing is new. Man is born, man lives, man dies. Nothing is new. What then is the point of life? What brings meaning to any person's life? Solomon wanted to know, so he set about to discover this, seeking wisdom.

∾∾∾

DAY ONE

We'll begin by reading Ecclesiastes 1 all the way through without stopping to mark or make notes. Simply get the flavor of this opening chapter.

Now read through Ecclesiastes 1 again and put a blue circle around every reference to the author. List what you learn about him by marking these references and by asking the 5 W's and an H.

The author of every book in the Bible emphasizes subjects by repeating key words and phrases. You'll be marking many of these throughout Ecclesiastes, so as we suggested in "How to Get Started," record them and how you plan to mark them on a three-by-five card you can use for a bookmark. Doing this from lesson to lesson will help you mark consistently and will save you time.

Now read through Ecclesiastes 1 and mark *vanity*.[1] The

Hebrew word (*hebel*) is used 38 times in Ecclesiastes and is translated *vanity* or *futility* most of the time in the NASB. Its literal meaning is breath or vapor, so it can be a metaphor for something that is fleeting, temporary, empty, senseless, or worthless, depending on the context. Although *futility* is not used in this chapter, you'll want to mark it and *vanity* the same way throughout the book. Also mark the synonymous phrase *striving after wind*[2] the same way.

DAY TWO

In your first readings of Ecclesiastes 1, you may have noticed the repeated phrases *under the sun* and *under heaven*. Read through the chapter again and mark these two phrases the same way. Also mark the key words *wisdom* and *folly*.

Now list what you learned about each of these words and phrases.

DAY THREE

Now that you've observed the chapter, it's time to think about its meaning. The goal of interpretation is to understand the message so you can apply it to your life. So, what did the Preacher ("Teacher" in the NIV) mean by "vanity"?

Let's look at the chapter a few verses at a time. What is the subject of verses 3-11? Now look at what the Preacher says in verses 12-18. How is he going to discover "all that has been done under heaven"? Is this a good way to learn what he wants to know?

Does it sound depressing? What is his point? Well, the answer isn't apparent in chapter 1. It will take a few more chapters to discover what the Preacher means about this in the first chapter. The key is what the Preacher knows about God.

Now, think about all you have seen these last three days and determine the main subject of this chapter. Write this out as a theme for Ecclesiastes 1 and record it on ECCLESIASTES AT A GLANCE on page 51.

DAY FOUR

Let's move on to chapter 2 today, keeping in mind what we thought about yesterday, and see if we can discover clues in this chapter to help us understand the Preacher better. Read through Ecclesiastes 2 and mark the key words and phrases you marked in chapter 1. Also mark *labor*,[3] *fate*,[4] and references to *God*.

DAY FIVE

List what you learn about *vanity, folly, labor, wisdom* and *God* in Ecclesiastes 2. Making lists is a key tool of careful observation. As you look at each place you marked a key word, ask the 5 W's and an H, and let the text provide the answers.

Also list what the Preacher says he did (the activities he engaged in) and the results.

DAY SIX

Now let's put together what we learned from chapters 1–2 about the Preacher's understanding of wisdom, labor, and vanity. What kind of wisdom (or whose wisdom) is vanity? What kind of labor (or whose labor) is vanity? How does God fit into man's labor and wisdom?

Read Proverbs 1:7; 2:6; 3:13; 4:5; 9:10; 15:33. If you haven't studied Proverbs, you need to know that wisdom is a central theme of the book and Solomon was its principal author. Would Solomon have been likely to mean one thing in Proverbs and something else entirely in Ecclesiastes? Or was he more likely to have been consistent? Remember, Scripture never contradicts Scripture.

Read 1 Corinthians 1:18-24.

Considering the verses in Proverbs and 1 Corinthians, are all labor and all wisdom vanity, or is the Preacher referring only to a certain kind of labor and wisdom?

Finally, thinking about all you have seen, what's the main subject of Ecclesiastes 2? Write this out as a chapter theme and record it on ECCLESIASTES AT A GLANCE on page 51.

DAY SEVEN

  Store in your heart: Ecclesiastes 2:25
Read and discuss: Ecclesiastes 1–2

QUESTIONS FOR DISCUSSION OR INDIVIDUAL STUDY

- ✴ Discuss what you learned about the author in Ecclesiastes 1–2.

- ✴ Discuss the relationship between labor and vanity.

- ✴ What did you learn about wisdom?

- How does God fit into the Preacher's eva
  of labor and wisdom? What part does God
  man's labor?

- What can you apply to your own life? What's your
  perspective on your own labor?

Thought for the Week

One of man's most common desires is to feel appreciated, to know that what he does is worthwhile and valuable. Solomon addresses this idea but in a very surprising way. It's somewhat shocking to see him despairing, dejected, and depressed. The first impression you get is that he is completely frustrated with life.

Sometimes we're frustrated because our perspective is flawed. When we stop to evaluate things, we realize that the thing we're frustrated about is not really the issue. The real problem is with our perspective—it needs adjusting. For Solomon the Preacher, the perspective that mattered the most was not his own, but God's.

If we look at Paul's first letter to the church in Corinth, we learn the difference between worldly wisdom (man's wisdom) and wisdom from above (God's wisdom). The world's wisdom is inadequate for knowing God: "For since in the wisdom of God the world through its wisdom did not *come to* know God..." (1 Corinthians 1:21).

In verse 24, we learn that Christ, who is preached in the gospel, is both the power of God and the wisdom of God. Yes, Christ Himself is the wisdom of God. That's why Jesus told His disciples that something greater than Solomon had arrived (Matthew 12:42). He was referring to Himself. Solomon, who was given great wisdom by God, was less than Jesus, who is God's wisdom.

Because of this, faith in Jesus as the Son of God, our Savior, is faith in the power and wisdom of God. That faith does not rest on man's wisdom, but on the power of God. It rests on the person of Jesus Christ.

And so when we share the gospel, 1 Corinthians 2:6-8 says we speak wisdom "not of this age nor of the rulers of this age," but "God's wisdom in a mystery, the hidden wisdom which God predestined before the ages to our glory, the wisdom which none of the rulers of this age has understood."

First Corinthians 2:14 goes on to inform us that "a natural man does not accept the things of the Spirit of God, for they are foolishness to him; and he cannot understand them, because they are spiritually appraised." So God's wisdom is different from man's in several respects. First, it is not understood by the natural man, including the rulers of this age. It is a mystery, hidden from men. Understanding comes only from enlightenment. Second, this wisdom precedes man, having been predestined before the ages. It exists apart from man.

So Solomon evaluates man's unaided efforts to understand God's wisdom and determines they are futile, and Paul tells us God's wisdom was a mystery, it was hidden, and it was not understood. Man can't understand God's wisdom without the Spirit of God. Solomon received wisdom from God, and he knew that man's attempt to understand wisdom on his own is vanity, even "vanity of vanities."

Furthermore, if God's wisdom is beyond man's wisdom, mysterious and hidden, then two things are vain: man's effort to gain God's wisdom and man's wisdom itself.

Now, let's be clear that the subject at hand is wisdom. If wisdom is knowledge that is applied rightly, then the subject is the right application of knowledge, not only the knowledge itself. In Ecclesiastes, Solomon examines man's quest for wisdom apart from God. And he rightly declares that this effort and its product, human wisdom, are vain.

There's a Time for Everything

Every event under heaven has an appointed time. But what about eternity? Time is the measure of things on earth, but eternity is beyond time. Forever transcends time. So we measure our lives on earth in time quantities, but we measure our life in heaven only in quality.

DAY ONE

Read through Ecclesiastes 3 today, marking the key words on your bookmark and references to *time*. When the Word of God gives us time indicators, we need to pay attention. There are a few time references in Ecclesiastes 3, such as *forever* and *eternity*, but most often the word *time* itself will be the key to understanding another key principle Solomon is bringing to light. Mark references to *time* with a clock, like this:

DAY TWO

List the things that there is a time for. Note the contrasts. Also list what you learn about eternity. Remember, ask the 5 W's and an H as you do this.

Also list what you learn about God.

21

DAY THREE

What does Ecclesiastes 3 reveal about the task God has given men on earth?

Read Ecclesiastes 3:16-22 and mark *wicked(ness)* and *righteous(ness)*. Add *wicked* to your bookmark. List what you learn about wickedness, righteousness, and God's judgment.

Finally, determine a theme for Ecclesiastes 3 and record it on ECCLESIASTES AT A GLANCE on page 51.

DAY FOUR

Read Ecclesiastes 4 today and mark the key words on your bookmark. Mark *evil* the same way you marked *wicked*.

DAY FIVE

Now list what you learn from marking *under the sun, vanity,* and *labor*. Think carefully about the principles you learn here about labor. What are good motives and what are not? What is the value of working together?

Get more done – Enjoy life [handwritten]

Strength [handwritten]

Work hard but enter moderation [handwritten margin note]

DAY SIX

Read Proverbs 12:24; 13:11; 14:23 and compare these to what you have learned about labor in Ecclesiastes.

What did you learn about the "poor yet wise lad"? How does this compare to what you learned about wisdom earlier in Ecclesiastes?

Hard workers become leaders [handwritten margin note]

little by little [handwritten margin note]

Profit [handwritten margin note]

So far, what would you say is Solomon's view of labor and its results? Is he a pessimist, or does he see an alternative to the labor that is vanity? How does this relate to time and eternity?

Don't forget to determine a theme for Ecclesiastes 4 and record it on ECCLESIASTES AT A GLANCE on page 51.

DAY SEVEN

Store in your heart: Ecclesiastes 3:1

Read and discuss: Ecclesiastes 3–4

QUESTIONS FOR DISCUSSION OR INDIVIDUAL STUDY

- ∾ Discuss the things and events that have appointed times. What is Solomon's point?

- ∾ Contrast time and eternity. How do they relate to vanity?

- ∾ What did you learn about wickedness, righteousness, and judgment?

- ∾ Discuss what you learned about labor—its value and results as well as workers' motives.

- ∾ What did you learn about happiness?

- ∾ Discuss any proverbs you discovered in Ecclesiastes 3–4.

THOUGHT FOR THE WEEK

Fans of 1960s folk-rock music may remember the hit song

"Turn, Turn, Turn" made famous by the Byrds. Other than the song's last lines ("I swear it's not too late"), which refers to "a time for peace," the lyrics are taken verbatim from the King James Version of Ecclesiastes 3:1-8. Many of us who are old enough to have listened to that song way back then didn't know it was from Scripture, but I find it interesting that the Word of God played so prominent a role in the counterculture of rock and roll and the antiwar movement in the Vietnam war era.

The song protested the Vietnam war and pled for peace, as if that were the main point of the Scripture passage. Taken out of context, words can be made to say just about anything, bent to serve the purpose of someone other than the original author. Solomon, of course, didn't get credit for the lyrics of this popular song. Nor did God get the glory for the true meaning of the passage.

When we look at the 28 items in verses 2-8 that have appointed times, we see that they touch many different areas of life by means of seven contrasts, each repeated with typical Hebrew parallelism. Look at verse 2 for example: "A time to give birth" is contrasted with "a time to die." In the next line, "a time to plant" is contrasted with "a time to uproot what is planted." But this is a parallel restatement of the first idea: "A time to plant" is "a time to give birth," and "a time to die" is "a time to uproot what is planted." There is one primary thought in the verse—a beginning and end to all things on earth. Each has its own life cycle. The idea is that *living things* last only for a time.

In the third verse, "a time to kill" is contrasted with "a time to heal," and "a time to tear down" is contrasted with "a time to build up." "Kill" parallels "tear down," and "heal" parallels "build up." The single idea is that everything *made by man* lasts only for a time.

Verse 4 teaches that we react to the transient nature of life and the fruit of our labors with weeping or laughter, sadness or joy, mourning or dancing. For example, we laugh and dance at birth, but we weep and mourn at death.

Verse 5 teaches us about labor—casting away stones and gathering stones. People often gathered stones to erect a monument, wall, or structure so they could build and protect their community life and individual lives. Casting stones away speaks of destruction, of tearing down what is not good. So we embrace and shun embracing, depending on the times.

Verse 6 gives us insight into value. We search for lost articles of value, but when we value our time more than the items we lose, we give up and accept the loss. So we possess or don't possess items based on their value; we keep them or throw them away. After things have served their purpose in their time, they may become useless to us.

Verse 7 reminds us that we need to speak at the right time, either to tear down what is false or injurious (that is, to confront error or evil) or to "sew together"—to mend or make what is good and right.

Finally, verse 8 brings us to the ultimate contrast between love and hate, which respectively produce peace and war. We live peaceably with those we love, and we fight the things we hate.

These seven couplets of contrasts can also be analyzed by grouping like words, something akin to the blessings and curses the Israelites recited on Mounts Ebal and Gerazim, as recorded in Deuteronomy 28. There are times for giving birth, planting, healing, building up, laughing, dancing, gathering stones, embracing, searching, keeping, sewing together, speaking, loving, and peace. And there are times for dying, uprooting, killing, tearing down, being silent, weeping, mourning, casting away stones, shunning embrace, giving up as lost, throwing away, tearing apart, hating, and war.

Now, just when do these times occur? Well, we have peace (and all those other things) when we are reconciled to God through our faith in the death, burial, and resurrection of Jesus Christ. In Solomon's day, this faith was placed in the promised seed. Abraham, for example, believed God's promises, and God counted him righteous.

We are called *now* to battle the principalities and powers of darkness that wage war against God. We are called to hate the sin that entangles and destroys us, keeping us from running the race toward victory. We tear down these things, tear them apart, and throw them away.

But what about speaking and being silent? James reminds us how difficult it is to tame the tongue—but we must. We must learn when to speak and when to remain silent. Jesus spoke for three years, but when His inquisitors abused Him at His trial, He was silent. He did not respond to them in kind. Like a lamb led to slaughter, He did not open His mouth. Yet He cried to God in His agony in Gethsemane and from the cross.

If we follow Christ's example of when to speak and when to be silent, and if we depend on God for justification and protection, knowing our circumstances are in His hand, we can have peace.

There is a time for every desire under heaven.

YOUR PURPOSE IN LIFE

Why do you work? Why do you worship? What are you trying to accomplish? Are you accumulating wealth? What will you do if you lose it all? Are you planning to take it with you when you die? Do you worship so you can get things?

DAY ONE

Read Ecclesiastes 5 today, marking the key words from your bookmark. *Emptiness*[5] is a synonym for *vanity*.

DAY TWO

What is the common subject in verses 1-9?
Read the following verses:

Leviticus 19:12

Numbers 30:2

Deuteronomy 23:21-23

1 Samuel 15:13-22

Malachi 1:7-14

Romans 12:1-2

What do these verses reveal about sacrifices and vows?

DAY THREE

What is the common subject in verses 10-20?
Read the following verses:

Job 1:21

Matthew 6:19-24

1 Timothy 6:10

Hebrews 13:5

Summarize what you learned about money and wealth.
Determine a theme for Ecclesiastes 5 and record it on
ECCLESIASTES AT A GLANCE on page 51.

DAY FOUR

Read Ecclesiastes 6 and mark the key words on your bookmark. Remember to mark *vanity, futility,* and *striving after the
wind* the same way since they are the same Hebrew word.

DAY FIVE

How do Ecclesiastes 6:1-2 connect to the last chapter? What
do you learn about God and wealth?

List what Solomon says about vanity and futility in this chapter. Note whether these things are part of temporal, earthly life or eternal life.

Read the following verses:

Job 8:9

Psalm 144:3-4

— Colossians 2:16-17

— Hebrews 8:4-5

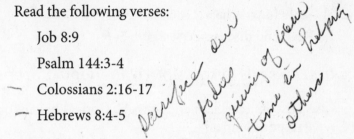

What did you learn about things on earth versus things in heaven?

DAY SIX

Some commentators divide the book of Ecclesiastes into two sections, the second beginning with 6:10. Think about the content of the first six chapters. Then read the following verses:

Ecclesiastes 6:10

Psalm 139:16

Proverbs 20:24

Acts 4:27-28

Romans 8:29-30

1 Corinthians 2:7-9

What light do these verses shed on Solomon's statement that "whatever exists has already been named"?

Finally, determine a theme for Ecclesiastes 6 and record it on ECCLESIASTES AT A GLANCE on page 51.

DAY SEVEN

💟 Store in your heart: Ecclesiastes 5:19
   Read and discuss: Ecclesiastes 5–6

QUESTIONS FOR DISCUSSION OR INDIVIDUAL STUDY

- ∾ Discuss sacrifices and vows to God. What are our responsibilities?

- ∾ Discuss wealth and riches. What should our attitude toward them be?

- ∾ In what ways is life on this earth a shadow? How does this fit with what you've seen in previous chapters about times and eternity?

- ∾ Discuss what you learned about things God ordained (predestined). How does this connect eternity to life on earth?

- ∾ To summarize this section of Ecclesiastes, what have you learned? What is Solomon's "great question" about life? Does he hint at an answer?

THOUGHT FOR THE WEEK

In Romans 12:1, Paul urges his readers, "Present your bodies a living and holy sacrifice, acceptable to God, which is your spiritual service of worship." This is not a new topic for the Bible. It dates back to Cain and Abel, the sons of Adam and Eve. Abel sacrificed according to God's will, but Cain didn't. When Cain saw that Abel's sacrifice pleased God, he didn't bring a new and acceptable offering to please God. Instead, he murdered Abel.

God told the first king of Israel, Saul, to completely destroy the Amalekites and their animals for their unprovoked attack on Israel. But Saul chose instead to capture their king and leave the best of the flocks and herds alive. When God's prophet Samuel challenged him about his conduct, Saul excused himself by saying the animals were for sacrifice to God. In response, Samuel reinforced the principle from the story of Cain and Abel:

> Has the LORD as much delight in burnt
>   offerings and sacrifices
> As in obeying the voice of the LORD?
> Behold, to obey is better than sacrifice,
> And to heed than the fat of rams.
> For rebellion is as the sin of divination,
> And insubordination is as iniquity and
>   idolatry (1 Samuel 15:22-23).

Many generations later, Malachi reprimanded Israel for offering sick and lame animals rather than the unblemished ones God required. Even an earthly governor, he said, would not accept such a sacrifice, and God called the offering evil. In fact, this account highlights the idea of sacrifice. An offering isn't a sacrifice if it has no value to you. If it's not something you can sell, if it's trash, it's not a sacrifice. Only something valuable is a sacrifice. Sacrifice implies loss: less money, time, or life.

Cain, Saul, and the Israelites of Malachi's time had the same problem with their offerings. God didn't accept them because they were made out of disobedience. None of them were *true* sacrifices. Cain's sacrifice was cheap, Saul's was ill-gotten gain, and the Jews in Malachi's day offered castoffs.

So what does this mean for you and me? How should we obey Romans 12:1? What *is* an acceptable sacrifice, a spiritual service of worship? What should be sacrificed? Paul gives us the answer: We are to offer our bodies as living and holy sacrifices. Our lives are to be holy as God is holy. As living sacrifices, we don't physically die as Jesus did, but we sacrifice our lives to God. We live not for ourselves but for Him. Whatever we do is to be done in a holy manner and for the Lord.

There is no vanity in this, no striving after wind, no futility. This life is not meaningless. People struggle every day to learn the meaning of life, as Solomon did according to these first six chapters. The answer to meaning is found in a holy life of service to God.

cht 7-8,

Who Knows What Is Good for a Man During His Lifetime?

Solomon asks a key question at the end of chapter 6, and he starts his answer in chapter 7. Man may not know what is good for him, but God knows. God is in control.

DAY ONE

Read Ecclesiastes 7 and mark the key words on your bookmark. Remember to ask the 5 W's and an H so you're reading with a purpose. Think about what you're reading as you go.

DAY TWO

List in your notebook what you learned about *wisdom, fools, the wicked, the righteous,* and *God.* There are many wonderful nuggets of truth in this chapter, like the ones you find in Proverbs.

DAY THREE

Today let's see if we can apply what we learn. Read Ecclesiastes 7:23-29 again and mark *discover*[6] but don't add it to your bookmark (it occurs only in chapters 7 and 8). What has Solomon been trying to discover? What has he found out, and what has he not found out?

What is the immediate subject in these few verses? Is there a broader context? Review what you learned about wise men and fools.

Finally, determine a theme for chapter 7 and add it to ECCLESIASTES AT A GLANCE.

DAY FOUR

Today, read through Ecclesiastes 8, marking the key words from your bookmark. Keep asking the 5 W's and an H. Keep in mind what you've already read and recorded about the key words.

DAY FIVE

Make lists of what you learn from marking key words. Remember that what you list will answer the 5 W's and an H.

DAY SIX

Read Ecclesiastes 8:16-17 again and mark *discover*.[7] Now list what you learned about this word, and compare your findings to what you listed from chapter 7.

What did Solomon seek to know? What did he discover that gave him his answer? What was his answer? How does this strike you? This chapter includes several things that seem contradictory, but it also includes one truth about God that leads you to the answer. What is that truth?

Does "the king" represent God in this chapter? What parallels between God and a human king are here?

According to what you've been reading, is God in control even when circumstances don't seem right to you? How can this truth help you?

Don't forget to record a theme for Ecclesiastes 8 on ECCLESIASTES AT A GLANCE.

DAY SEVEN

Store in your heart: Ecclesiastes 8:12

Read and discuss: Ecclesiastes 7–8

QUESTIONS FOR DISCUSSION OR INDIVIDUAL STUDY

∾ What did you learn about wisdom and fools?

∾ What does Solomon try to discover, and what does he learn?

∾ How do the truths of these chapters relate to the questions at the end of chapter 6? Who is stronger than man (6:10)? Who knows what is good for a man? Who can tell a man what will be after him under the sun (6:12)? Discuss these; don't give one-word answers.

∾ Discuss how you can apply what you learned in Ecclesiastes 7–8 to your life today.

THOUGHT FOR THE WEEK

Who knows what is good for man? Does any man know? Does King Solomon? Or was this knowledge beyond him even though he was the wisest man on earth? Solomon's wisdom led him to this conclusion: Man should consider the work of God.

God is in control. Even when circumstances are unjust, God is in control. He gives us both prosperity and adversity—neither is ultimately the work of our hands. We may labor, but God determines the outcome. And because God is in control and our prosperity is His gift, we cannot know what God will do with it. As Job said, "The LORD gave and the LORD has taken away. Blessed be the name of the LORD."

In Ecclesiastes 6:12, Solomon asks, "Who knows what is good for a man?" The answer is, God! God knows what is best for each of us. He graciously gives us what we need but not always what we ask for. If we don't ask according to God's will, we don't need it! We don't always need comfort, ease, and pleasure. We may have these things at times, but we must remember that God has granted them according to His will. But what we actually need is to be conformed to the image of His Son. James said it this way:

> Consider it all joy, my brethren, when you encounter various trials, knowing that the testing of your faith produces endurance. And let endurance have its perfect result, so that you may be perfect and complete, lacking in nothing (James 1:2-4).

God has made provision for us so we are "lacking in nothing." That provision is not found in prosperity, but in trial. That's because He's perfecting our character, not our finances. Note how the phrase "lacking in nothing" qualifies the phrase "perfect and complete," which of course refers to our character, not our money.

Jesus emphasized God's concern for our needs in His Sermon on the Mount. He told us that God knows all our needs and that we should seek God's kingdom and righteousness first, confident that He will supply all our needs: food, drink, and clothing. Jesus even refers to Solomon, who despite all his glory could not clothe himself the way God clothes the lilies of the field.

Solomon knew God provides material things. And he even knew God provides forgiveness of sins to those who fear Him. Solomon also realized that good things don't always happen to good people or bad things to bad people. He's seen the wicked prosper and the righteous suffer. But according to chapter 8, he knows that ultimately, "it will be well for those who fear God, who fear Him openly." Solomon is so convinced of this that he would not change his mind even if a sinner did evil 100 times and was somehow able to prolong his life. First John 1:9 says, "If we confess our sins, He is faithful and righteous to forgive us our sins and to cleanse us from all unrighteousness."

Evil men don't confess their sins because they don't fear God. They won't call sin "sin," and they don't acknowledge that God righteously judges sin. So they won't receive forgiveness. Regardless of material prosperity in this life under the sun, the end of the wicked will be just because God is just.

(Search bar wisdom)

Fear God & follow his commandments

WISDOM IS BETTER THAN STRENGTH

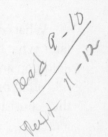

The book of Proverbs, which Solomon also wrote, contrasts wisdom and folly, the wise man and the fool. These chapters of Ecclesiastes do the same. What advantage does wisdom give us? Don't fools also prosper?

DAY ONE

Read Ecclesiastes 9, marking the key words from your bookmark. Mark *love* but don't add it to your bookmark. Ask as many of the 5 W's and an H as you can think of! Stay engaged with the text. Don't fall into the trap of mindless marking.

DAY TWO

Today list what you learned from marking key words in Ecclesiastes 9. Note any contrasts because they're intended to help us understand truth.

DAY THREE

What conclusions can you draw from Ecclesiastes 9 about fate? What happens to all men? Because of this fate, how does Solomon advise us to live? What principles does he give us?

What principles about wisdom does Solomon give? Are they consistent with all you've learned for the last eight chapters?

Finally, determine a theme for Ecclesiastes 9 and record it on ECCLESIASTES AT A GLANCE.

DAY FOUR

Today read Ecclesiastes 10 and, as usual, mark the key words from your bookmark.

DAY FIVE

List what you learned from marking key words in Ecclesiastes 10. Notice the great contrast between wisdom and foolishness in this chapter. You might want to make a two-column chart to list, compare, and contrast what you learned about these two key concepts.

DAY SIX

Compare Ecclesiastes 10:14 with 6:12. What answer to the question at hand has Solomon discovered?

How would you describe Solomon's tone in 10:19? Is Solomon qualifying verses 16 and 18 in some way? Remember, parallelism is a characteristic of Hebrew poetry; sometimes a verse is parallel to the one before it, restating its truth. What is Solomon's view of the fool?

What advantage does wisdom have? Give some examples from the chapter.

Finally, determine a theme for Ecclesiastes 10 and record it on ECCLESIASTES AT A GLANCE.

DAY SEVEN

 Store in your heart: Ecclesiastes 10:12
Read and discuss: Ecclesiastes 9–10

QUESTIONS FOR DISCUSSION OR INDIVIDUAL STUDY

- Discuss the contrast of wisdom and folly (the wise man and the fool) in these two chapters.

- Discuss man's common fate. What difference does it make if a man is wise or foolish?

- What kind of life does Solomon recommend based on man's fate? Could he have advised another kind of life? What makes the difference?

- What did you learn about God in these chapters? How should we live our lives in light of this?

- What else can you apply to your own life?

THOUGHT FOR THE WEEK

Solomon declares in chapter 9 that "righteous men, wise men, and their deeds are in the hand of God." Not everyone accepts this powerful truth. Some say it's fatalistic, that we're mere puppets in the hands of a cosmic puppet master. Given this view, they think they have no responsibility for their actions and can't be held accountable. As a result, they deny God's judgment.

The opposite view is that we control our lives and make our own destinies, that we determine our own futures by the way we live, good or bad. Some people believe we accumulate karma (good and bad works) that determines ongoing reincarnations. Of course, the Bible teaches nothing close to reincarnation, but in Galatians 6:7, Paul does emphasize that our actions bring consequences: "Whatever a man sows, this he will also reap."

So what's the truth? Do we control our lives, or does God? The answer is, both. God says we reap what we sow. In New Testament terms, if we sow to the flesh, we reap corruption, but if we sow to the Spirit, we reap eternal life (Galatians 6:8). The apostle Paul sets this truth in a context of sharing what we have with those who teach us good things. You can selfishly spend on yourself, but what will be your reward? In Solomon's words, nothing else under the sun. Earthly treasures are not ultimately valuable because they will not last. As Jesus said in the Sermon on the Mount, moths eat them, rust destroys them, and thieves steal them. If you sow to the Spirit, giving with thankfulness for the truth of God's Word that saves you, you are seeking treasure in heaven, which lasts.

Solomon's main idea in Ecclesiastes 9 is that we can spend our lives on the pleasures of this life or on eternal things. Solomon doesn't speak about eternal life in Ecclesiastes. He does say that God is in control and that we should live under

His sovereignty rather than the sovereignty of fools. Wisdom turns our hearts toward God in gratitude for what He has given us in this life—things that we can freely enjoy.

As he does in the book of Proverbs, Solomon dispenses advice for wise living. He understands that there are both wise and foolish choices in life, and it's better to make the wise ones. Wisdom, as he has outlined it before, acknowledges that God is in control and therefore acknowledges God in all things. We don't know what lies ahead in this life. Circumstances may be pleasant or painful. We may be rich or poor, healthy or sick, strong or weak.

Solomon gives us a part of the picture but not the whole picture. He stops short of saying what we learn elsewhere in the Bible—that those who believe the gospel know their eternal future. Each day surprises us one way or the other, but God's Holy Word assures us that our future is secure in heaven. We can read about Jesus coming for us, about being changed, and about the new heaven and earth.

Paul contrasts foolishness and wisdom in 1 Corinthians and shows us that God uses the foolish things of the world to shame the wise of the world. Jesus is "the wisdom of God" (1 Corinthians 1:24). Solomon didn't write about eternity; he looked only at life on earth and tried to understand what he saw. He understood this: Righteous and wise men and their deeds are in the hand of God. If nothing else, Solomon understood God's providence, and so he wrote about living this life under the sun but also under the sovereignty of God. And this he called wisdom.

ASHES TO ASHES, DUST TO DUST

What happens when we die? Do we have a future and a hope? Will we be reincarnated? The world has many answers, but the Bible has the truth. What does Ecclesiastes tell us? What wisdom does Solomon bring us from God?

DAY ONE

Read Ecclesiastes 11, marking the key words on your bookmark. Don't miss time phrases that relate to the times of life.

DAY TWO

Read Ecclesiastes 11:1-6 again. Each verse is a proverb about life, but there is a common thread. Who is in charge? Summarize this paragraph.

Read Deuteronomy 15:9-10 and Matthew 5:42 and think about how these verses shed light on Ecclesiastes 11:1-2.

What principles can you draw from verses 3-6?

DAY THREE

Read Ecclesiastes 11:7-10. List in your notebook what you learn from each of the phrases related to the seasons of life.

Is Solomon advocating a licentious lifestyle? Is he suggesting you live it up because everything is futile? Remember to keep things in context. What principle did you learn from verse 9?

What contrasts with *rejoice* in these verses? What did you learn about God in this chapter that will help you understand how to live?

Lastly, determine a theme for Ecclesiastes 11 and record it on ECCLESIASTES AT A GLANCE.

DAY FOUR

Read Ecclesiastes 12. Mark the key words from your bookmark and pay attention to time phrases. Verses 1-4 are one long sentence. How do the time phrases connect chapters 11 and 12? How do these verses describe old age?

DAY FIVE

Read verses 5-8 in light of what you looked at in verses 1-4. How do they relate? What is man's end?

Read the following verses:

Genesis 2:7   *Made Man from dust*

Genesis 3:19   *Made from dust*
               return to dust

Psalm 104:29-30

Ecclesiastes 3:19-21

Philippians 1:21-25

2 Corinthians 5:6-8

One of the great hopes we have is that our bodies will someday be transformed. Read 1 Corinthians 15:35-57 and note why we can face the aging process with hope.

DAY SIX

Finally, read Ecclesiastes 12:9-14 and summarize what the Preacher was doing in this book.

What does he conclude? Summarize this chapter and record this theme on ECCLESIASTES AT A GLANCE.

Now, looking at all the chapter themes you've recorded on ECCLESIASTES AT A GLANCE, determine an overall theme for the book and record it. All the chapter themes should relate to this book theme in some way, explaining one or more aspects of the overall message. Remember to use words from texts if you can—phrases or portions of verses are good tools to use.

DAY SEVEN

Store in your heart: Ecclesiastes 12:13-14
Read and discuss: Ecclesiastes 11–12

QUESTIONS FOR DISCUSSION OR INDIVIDUAL STUDY

- ∾ Discuss generosity and giving from Ecclesiastes 11.

- ∾ What truths did you learn about God in these chapters that are key to living a life of faith?

- ∾ Discuss the aging process described in Ecclesiastes 11–12. How does the Preacher say we are to live each stage of life?

- ∾ Relate your experiences to these stages of life. What has been your attitude so far? Do these chapters challenge you to do anything for the rest of your life?

- ∾ Discuss the value of wisdom. Feel free to go back over anything you learned in the entire book of Ecclesiastes.

- ∾ What is man's end? What happens to his body? His spirit? What happens in the resurrection?

THOUGHT FOR THE WEEK

"Ashes to ashes; dust to dust" is often heard at burials because the earthly body we inhabit is perishable. God made the first man's body from the dust of the earth, and as a consequence of Adam's sin, his body eventually returned to the dust of the earth. We're all mortals. Our bodies eventually die. Usually they're either buried (where they decompose) or they're cremated. Ashes to ashes, dust to dust.

Life is always defined by when it starts—the instant of conception, when breathing begins, or when an unborn baby is first able to survive outside the womb. Similarly, death happens when something ends—a heartbeat, breathing, or brain activity. But these medical definitions relate only to physical life. They have nothing to do with the spirit God gave.

Of course, some deny that there is life after death, or an afterlife. They deny that any part of man lives on. But Ecclesiastes 12:7 says the spirit returns to God, who gave it.

Paul says Christians who die are absent from the body and present with the Lord (2 Corinthians 5:6-9). As he had already explained to the Corinthian church, the perishable cannot inherit the imperishable (1 Corinthians 15:50). It cannot live forever in its current state. So in the resurrection, our bodies will be raised in a form that lives forever. We don't know what they will look like, but we know they will have characteristics needed for heavenly living. (Paul does give us one hint: Christ was raised as "the first fruits of those who are asleep," so our resurrection bodies may be like His.)

Writing to the Thessalonian church, Paul said that those who sleep in Christ (those who are believers whose bodies have died) will rise, and we who are alive will be caught up together with them in the clouds to meet the Lord in the air and always be with the Lord (1 Thessalonians 4:15-18). Our bodies will change in the twinkling of an eye (1 Corinthians 15:52). So both the Old and New Testaments tell us we will live on.

Jesus told the story of a rich man who died and was in a place of torment after his death. From there he saw Abraham and cried out for relief. Receiving none, he wanted to send a message to his brothers so they wouldn't end up like him. Abraham responded that if people alive don't listen to Moses and the prophets, they won't be persuaded by someone who rises from the dead (Luke 16:19-31). People who despise God's law and prophecies are not convinced that Jesus has risen from the dead.

The main point of the resurrection of the righteous and the

wicked (Acts 24:15) is that life continues after the body dies; eternal destinies are real. Revelation describes a second death, the lake of fire, in which those who do not believe the gospel spend eternity. But this death is not the cessation of breathing, heartbeats, or brain activities. This death lasts forever in torment, in contrast to the life forever with Christ.

This eternal life is the hope set before us—that after this earthly body dies, we have eternal life in the spirit immediately and a renewed, spiritual, immortal body when the Lord returns. And if we are alive when He returns for believers who have died, our bodies will be changed then. This gives us hope and comfort.

This is what Jesus lived and died for—to give those who believe in Him eternal life.

Theme of Ecclesiastes:

SEGMENT DIVISIONS

		CHAPTER THEMES	Author:

				Author:
		1	Man should enjoy his	Date:
chapter 3		2	Work	
		3	When mans work is	Purpose:
chap 4		4	Vanity is meaningless	Key Words:
		5		
		6	Who knows what is good for a	
				mas life
		7	Walk in the middle of foolishness	
		8	Chapter 8 - We 12	+ wisdom
		9		
		10		
		11		
		12		

SONG OF SOLOMON

INTRODUCTION TO
SONG OF SOLOMON

∽∽∽∽

The Song of Solomon records how Solomon understood love. Some think it represents Israel's relationship to God; others, the church's relationship to Jesus; others, the believer's relationship to Jesus; and still others, simply a love story between Solomon and his bride. But in every interpretation the lessons are about love—love between God and man and between a man and a woman.

Before we can interpret poetry, we must determine how the writer was using language. Was he using imagery to point to deeper realities, or was he speaking plainly and describing what actually happened? A literal approach simplifies the process of interpretation because it takes things at face value. Reading this way, we do not search for hidden meanings. If we read Song of Solomon as we would any other literature, seeking the author's meaning from the plain sense he expresses himself in, we'll come face-to-face with the love Solomon had for a woman and her love for him.

Still, Solomon does use imagery to describe the bride and bridegroom. These metaphors would have been clearly understood in Israel's culture in Solomon's day. Today, roughly 3000 years later, the images require some interpretation.

Song of Solomon is written almost like a play with dialogues for several characters, so to understand it, you'll need to identify who is speaking in each part. Many Bibles identify these parts for you. For example, the New American Standard Bible includes marginal notes that say "Bride," "Bridegroom," and "Chorus." If your Bible doesn't show these or if you like to discover as much as possible by yourself, when you read a passage, try to determine whether the bride, the bridegroom, or the chorus is speaking.

Solomon enjoyed love's wonder. He knew the intoxicating spell love has on a man and a woman, and he described it in vivid language. As we explore the love story in this short book and remember that the love between a man and a woman should be a reflection of the love between God and us, we will learn valuable principles for our lives.

How Beautiful You Are

Do you tell the one you love how beautiful she is or how handsome he is? If you're married or engaged, how do you express your love? Solomon tells us how he feels toward the woman he loves and how she feels toward him. And what an example it is!

DAY ONE

Read Song of Solomon 1 today without stopping. Just explore the language of this unique book of the Bible.

Now, read it over again and see if you can discern the characters—which verses each one speaks. Watch the pronouns for clues. What does the bride say to the bridegroom? How does he address her?

During your third pass through, divide the passages with a horizontal line and write in the margin who is speaking.

DAY TWO

Read Song of Solomon 1 again. This time mark *bride, bridegroom,* and the key words *love* and *beautiful.*[8] Add these to your bookmark. As you do, remember to ask the 5 W's and an H. Try to understand the flow of thought.

DAY THREE

List the bride's description of her bridegroom, the bridegroom's description of his bride, and the bride's description of herself.

The bridegroom says his bride is like a mare and her eyes are like a dove. This is complimentary imagery from the culture of the day. Look at the "mare" description more closely. What quality does he extol?

What characteristic of doves does he ascribe to her eyes?

The bride compares the bridegroom to a pouch of myrrh and a cluster of henna blossoms in the vineyards of Engedi. Myrrh is a fragrant spice, and Engedi is a beautiful oasis near the Dead Sea. The language invokes the geography of the area, but what does she mean? He is like them but in what way? What qualities does she have in mind?

What does the bride think of her own appearance? Whom is she addressing? Whose opinion is she concerned about? Who are "the daughters of Jerusalem"?

Now determine a theme for Song of Solomon 1 and record it on SONG OF SOLOMON AT A GLANCE on page 80. What is this first chapter about?

DAY FOUR

As you read today, remember that the Bible was not written in chapters. Read Song of Solomon 1:15 through 2:17 as if there were no chapter break. Mark the key words from your bookmark on this first reading. Also mark the key word *come* and add it to your bookmark.

DAY FIVE

Read Song of Solomon 2 again today and draw horizontal lines between the sections that the bridegroom, the bride, and the chorus speak.

How do chapters 1 and 2 connect? Continue your lists of the bride and bridegroom's descriptions of each other.

DAY SIX

Now let's analyze the poetic imagery in Song of Solomon 2. What quality does a lily among thorns have? What quality does an apple tree among trees of the forest have? The answers are right there in the text.

What qualities does a gazelle or young stag have, climbing on the mountains, leaping on the hills?

In Israel, the winter is the rainy season. In spring, the rains stop, and what has looked brown and barren for months erupts in flowers even today. Like spring everywhere, it is the season for new life. The fig tree bears fruit in three seasons, and the first figs ripen in spring. How does this help you understand the bridegroom's call to his bride?

What characteristics of the dove does the bridegroom use in this chapter?

Reflect on the compliments these two lovers give. They express the best qualities they see in each other. Do you do that? How do you express your love?

Now, summarize the essence of this chapter and record this theme on SONG OF SOLOMON AT A GLANCE on page 80.

DAY SEVEN

Store in your heart: Song of Solomon 2:16
Read and discuss: Song of Solomon 1–2

QUESTIONS FOR DISCUSSION OR INDIVIDUAL STUDY

- Discuss the bride's description of the bridegroom. Note the qualities she expresses and how this expresses her love for him.

- Discuss the same things for the bridegroom's description of the bride.

- Discuss parallels this love story has with God and Israel, Christ and the church, and your relationship with Christ, if you see any.

- Leave time for members of your group to share how this lesson spoke to them about verbalizing love to their spouse or betrothed.

THOUGHT FOR THE WEEK

"My beloved is mine, and I am his," says Song of Solomon 2:16. And verse 4 says, "His banner over me is love." These phrases formed the basis of a praise chorus that became popular in the early 1970s. The song allegorized the Song of Solomon to describe the love between a Christian and Jesus Christ, his Savior. This has been a popular interpretation of Song of Solomon, and certainly there are many wonderful parallels that help us make powerful applications.

At face value, the Song of Solomon is a song of rejoicing for a loving relationship. The man and woman see wonderful qualities in each other and express them poetically. The images of flowers and animals paint vivid pictures that describe many admirable qualities. Flowers picture beauty, fragrance, and delicateness. They engage the senses of sight, smell, and touch. They contrast with thorns, which are ugly, have no fragrance, and are dangerously sharp. The stag leaping on mountains is strong, athletic, agile, and free.

And so the bride is beautiful, fragrant, and delicate to her bridegroom. The bridegroom is strong, athletic, agile, and free to his bride. They admire one another's qualities and tell others about them.

Then the chorus chimes in, singing of little foxes that ruin the blossoming vineyards. Watch out for things that can ruin the beauty and fruitfulness of this loving relationship! In your man-woman relationships, whether you're dating, engaged, or married, do you express the qualities of the one you love to others? Do you tell other people about the things you like about your betrothed or spouse? Are you so enamored that you can't help going on and on about him or her? That's the example given here. We see praise for the beloved expressed to other people and also directly to the beloved.

That's the example we need to follow. We need to tell our wives or husbands, our fiancés or fiancées these things. It feeds their self-esteem, their self-worth; it assures them that we value them above all others. And if we are their beloved, they value our opinion more than any others.

These first two chapters challenge us to express love and admiration with an example of unashamed love. God's design for love between man and woman (and remember, this song is about a bride and bridegroom—a man and woman who become husband and wife) includes praise for real qualities He has created. It's not enough to just do nice things for each other; words matter too. You don't have to be poetic and flowery. Most guys can't muster the words to do this anyway, and women don't speak this way either!

It's not the imagery or quantity of words that affirms our love for one another, but the sincerity and frequency. It can be as simple as "I love you." Our memories carry these words with us daily. We can rehearse them whenever we want. God made our brains work that way. Words bring up images in our minds as they did in Solomon's. And when the words are pleasant, fragrant, and loving, the images are too.

Make a decision today to say something loving to the one you love. And if you think there's an analogy in the Song of Solomon to Jesus the bridegroom and the church, His bride, make a decision today to say something loving to Jesus. Tell Him you love Him and why.

PASSIONATE LOVE

~~~~~

Most brides want their wedding day to be perfect. They plan a once-in-a-lifetime event, a memory they'll cherish forever. Bridegrooms usually aren't quite so enthusiastic, but they don't want to disappoint their brides, and because they love them, they want to please and impress them. Solomon was no exception. He loved his bride passionately. To what lengths would he go to show his love for her?

DAY ONE

Read Song of Solomon 3 and mark the key words from your bookmark. Don't miss the time reference.

Now read the chapter again and mark the sections according to speaker and subject. What's happening in the first four verses? How does this fit everything you've seen before? Remember, it's right before the wedding. Why is this happening?

DAY TWO

List features of the event described in Song of Solomon 3:6-11. What is the event?

Remember, Solomon is king of Israel and is wealthy beyond compare. How does this influence the entourage, the carriage, and his attire?

Compare Song of Solomon 3:5 with 2:7. Who is speaking, and why is the sentiment repeated? How does the event that begins in verse 6 explain why this is said and the timing?

Record a theme for Song of Solomon 3 on SONG OF SOLOMON AT A GLANCE on page 80.

DAY THREE

Now read and mark Song of Solomon 4. As usual, identify the speakers and the sections of the chapter each is speaking in.

DAYS FOUR & FIVE

Read chapter 4 again and list everything you learn about the bride. Take your time and savor the words of the bridegroom.

Note especially how she's addressed in verse 8. What has Solomon called her to this point? Remember what happened at the end of chapter 3. When does chapter 4 occur?

Since we're reading poetic imagery, don't just list facts like "eyes like a dove"; instead, record the qualities that the images portray.

Remember, every comparison is a compliment. Consider what would be pleasing and complimentary to a bride on her wedding night. Some background information might also be helpful:

- ‿ In the Middle East, most goats are black and most sheep are white.

- ‿ The color of ripe pomegranates is roughly rouge.

- ‿ Lebanon is famous for its fragrant cedars.

DAY SIX

Finally, how does the bride respond to her husband? When she refers to her garden, is she speaking literally or figuratively? If this is a metaphor (a figure of speech or poetic image), what is she referring to?

Remember, this is their wedding night, and physical love is expressed in poetic terms.

Well, that's it for this week, Beloved! Don't forget to record a theme for Song of Solomon 4 on SONG OF SOLOMON AT A GLANCE on page 80.

DAY SEVEN

 Store in your heart: Song of Solomon 4:10

Read and discuss: Song of Solomon 3–4

QUESTIONS FOR DISCUSSION OR INDIVIDUAL STUDY

- ‿ What did you learn about the wedding procession? Describe the elements and their significance.

- ‿ Discuss Solomon's description of his bride on their wedding night. Go through the various images one by one. Comment on the detail and passion of the description.

ↁ What application can you make? How does this example challenge or affirm your love for your spouse?

Thought for the Week

According to Middle Eastern customs in Solomon's day, the bridegroom prepared a place for the bride in his father's house. When the father determined the time was right, the bridegroom would go to get his bride, accompanied by the wedding party. Then in a great procession, he would bring the bride to his father's house for the ceremony. The richer the bridegroom, the grander the procession.

The Scriptures give scant glimpses into these ceremonies, so extrabiblical sources are needed. These sources shed great light on many things taught in Scripture and help us understand both Old and New Testaments, for Israel is described as the wife of God, and the church is called the bride of Christ.

Song of Solomon, focused on the love of bride and bridegroom, gives us the one clear description in the Bible of a wedding procession. According to some commentators, Solomon appears to come riding on a carriage in this procession. Others think the language also conveys the idea that he has prepared this carriage and escort to protect the most precious thing in his life, his betrothed. If this is the case, then this procession fits the grand scheme of the bridegroom's honor for her, consistent with his adulation and adoration in the previous and following chapters.

If Song of Solomon is also intended for us to understand God's love for His wife, Israel, and Christ's love for His bride, the church, then the picture is even more significant and the details more worthy of inspection. Consider first of all how much the bridegroom thinks of his bride to provide this magnificent procession.

Then think of Christ's protection of His church until the wedding feast takes place. He has legions of angels. He carries us to our wedding; we don't have to walk to get there. The means of transport are royal: silver, gold, and purple. He clothes us in His robes of righteousness.

The bride and groom are specially clothed for the wedding. Isaiah 61:10 expresses it this way:

> I will rejoice greatly in the LORD,
> My soul will exult in my God;
> For He has clothed me with garments
>   of salvation,
> He has wrapped me with a robe of
>   righteousness,
> As a bridegroom decks himself with a garland,
> And as a bride adorns herself with her jewels.

Ezekiel 16:11-12 reinforces the notion of jewels and crowns:

> I adorned you with ornaments, put bracelets on
> your hands and a necklace around your neck. I
> also put a ring in your nostril, earrings in your
> ears and a beautiful crown on your head.

The garland for the bridegroom may refer to the crown mentioned in verse 11. Sometimes crowns were gold; other times they were made from flowers.

Although the wedding feast lasted a week, the marriage was consummated the night of the wedding (as chapter 4 follows chapter 3). Among the books of the Bible, Song of Solomon uniquely describes the intimacy of love between a bride and bridegroom, bringing the normal physical relationships of marriage into the spotlight. Even if the book is allegorical and poetic, the language is real and down-to-earth, showing us that physical expression is part of God's design. The terms are not raunchy, crude, or vulgar, but rather uplifting and beautiful. That's the way God intended love to be. We should never think that physical expressions of love in the context of marriage are anything but beautiful and pleasing to God.

O BELOVED, WHERE ART THOU?

According to 1 Kings 11, Solomon eventually had 700 wives (princesses) and 300 concubines. According to Song of Solomon 6:8, Solomon already had 60 queens, 80 concubines, and "maidens without number." How does one bride fit into this harem?

DAY ONE

Read Song of Solomon 5, marking the key words from your bookmark and the speakers. Mark each speaker's words as you have done before.

DAY TWO

Read Song of Solomon 4:16–5:1. How do they relate? Does 5:1 fit more closely with chapter 4 or chapter 5? What happens starting in 5:2? What change do you see?

List the points of 5:2-8. How do Solomon's many wives help explain the story?

Read the following verses:

Genesis 2:23-24

Matthew 19:4-6

1 Corinthians 6:15-17

Ephesians 5:25-33

How does the last phrase of Song of Solomon 6:8 fit with God's design for "one man, one woman"?

Solomand Life in King

DAY THREE

What part does the chorus play in the dialogue?

List the bride's description of her beloved in chapter 5. How does it compare with his description of her in chapter 4?

Record a theme for Song of Solomon 5 on SONG OF SOLOMON AT A GLANCE.

DAY FOUR

Read Song of Solomon 6 today, marking the key words from your bookmark as usual. Again, identify the speakers and mark their words. How does chapter 6 relate to chapter 5?

DAYS FIVE & SIX

What is the chorus's question in chapter 6? Compare it to the question in 5:9.

What two things does the chorus want to know? this help them respond to the bride's request in 5:8?

What is her response this time?

List the bridegroom's description of the bride in Song of Solomon 6:4-9. How does it compare with his description in chapter 4? What part of the description is different, and how is it different? How could this contribute to the events of these two chapters?

What did the queens and concubines praise? What was the chorus's reaction to everyone's praise of the bride?

Finally, record a theme for Song of Solomon 6 on SONG OF SOLOMON AT A GLANCE.

DAY SEVEN

 Store in your heart: Song of Solomon 6:3

Read and discuss: Song of Solomon 5–6

QUESTIONS FOR DISCUSSION OR INDIVIDUAL STUDY

- ∞ Discuss the order of events in these chapters and their significance.

- ∞ How did the bride try to remedy the situation?

- ∞ Discuss Solomon's description of his "darling."

- ∞ Discuss the "one man, one woman" principle from Scripture.

- ∞ Allow time for sharing how this principle has worked or failed in your group members' marriages. This can be painful but healing. Be sensitive.

Thought for the Week

 God's design for marriage is one man, one woman. In Genesis 2, God created a suitable helper for Adam, made from his flesh and bone. The two were to become one flesh. After that, when there were mothers, fathers, and other women, God commanded man to leave his family and become one flesh with his wife.

Jesus reaffirmed this principle. When questioned why Moses granted certificates of divorce, Jesus answered that it was because of their hard hearts, but He also said it wasn't that way from the beginning. He quoted Genesis 2:24 to give full force to the principle.

The issue in Song of Solomon 5–6 is not divorce but rather the principle of "one man, one woman." When Solomon wrote Song of Solomon 6:8, he apparently had 60 queens and 80 concubines. Among these he called the one he addressed in his book his dove, his perfect one, unique, her mother's only daughter, praised by the queens and concubines. By the end of his life he had acquired "700 wives, princesses, and 300 concubines" (1 Kings 11:3).

Was it enough for the subject of his book to be so poetically praised, to be "unique"? One answer is given in 5:8. She was lovesick. She had her own room, as did all the queens. Solomon visited his wives when their turn came, or he sent for them. They didn't have multiple husbands, so they had to wait, sharing the man they loved with other women. God had commanded Israel's kings not to "multiply wives" (Deuteronomy 17:17) so the kings' hearts would not be turned away from Him. According to 1 Kings 11, Solomon's foreign wives did in fact turn his heart away to idol worship.

But even here in chapters 5–6 we see the king's heart turned away from worshipping God. If Solomon were worshipping God, he would have obeyed Him. A few generations earlier, the prophet Samuel rebuked King Saul when Saul failed to destroy *all* the Amalekites and their animals. Samuel told Saul that obedience is better than sacrifice. Since sacrifice is an outward act of worship, it's reasonable to infer that disobedience is not worshipping and that worship includes obedience.

Solomon disobeyed God by multiplying wives. He violated Deuteronomy 17:17, and more critically, he violated Genesis 2:24. He wasn't the only king to do this, for even David, the man "according to" God's heart, had nine wives. The consequence here is unfulfilled *mutual* love. This woman loved Solomon with her whole heart, but she had only a part of his. Consider what she calls him—"beloved…whom my soul loves"—and his words for her—"My darling, my bride." He describes her love as beautiful, much better than wine. But he doesn't love her with his whole heart. It wasn't even halfhearted love—she had only a tiny fraction of his heart.

This isn't God's design. Paul tells the Ephesians a man is to love his own (one) wife as himself—one man, one woman.

Jean

Feb 19th

Some Beauty Is
Only Skin Deep

Most of the praise in Song of Solomon goes to physical beauty. But what about inner beauty, or character? We know that physical beauty attracts, but does it sustain a relationship for a lifetime? Do we find any evidence in this book that there is more to a relationship than physical attraction?

DAY ONE

Read Song of Solomon 7 today, marking the key words from your bookmark and identifying the speakers and their words.

DAY TWO

List Solomon's praises for his bride in chapter 7, or add them to your previous list. When you're done, go over all you've recorded from the first six chapters to see if you can find praise for anything other than physical beauty. If so, make a separate list.

DAY THREE

Now list what you learn from the bride's praise for Solomon in chapter 7. And just as you reviewed the bridegroom's words yesterday, examine all that she has said for seven chapters. See what you can find that is not about his physical beauty.

Contrast the invitation she extends in chapter 7 to the scene of chapter 5 and the first two verses of chapter 6. What do you think is going on?

Now determine a theme for the chapter and record it on SONG OF SOLOMON AT A GLANCE.

DAY FOUR

Read Song of Solomon 8 and mark key words as usual. Also note the speakers and their words.

DAY FIVE

List what you learn from the bride's speeches in chapter 8. Is there anything in this chapter we haven't seen before? What is she referring to here—a current experience with Solomon or a flashback?

And what do you learn from the bridegroom?

DAY SIX

Review what you've seen in chapter 8, summarize it in a theme, and record it on SONG OF SOLOMON AT A GLANCE.

We've come to the end of this love story, so it's time to draw out a general theme for the entire book. You may want to review the Song of Solomon by reading it through in one sitting. What is the dominant message throughout? What key words stand out? These will help you determine a theme for the book. When you've settled on a main idea, record it on SONG OF SOLOMON AT A GLANCE.

DAY SEVEN

 Store in your heart: Song of Solomon 7:6

Read and discuss: Song of Solomon 7–8

QUESTIONS FOR DISCUSSION OR INDIVIDUAL STUDY

- ∾ Discuss your insights about Solomon's love for the Shulammite (as she's called in 6:13). Be sure to list what he loves her for.

- ∾ Also discuss your insights about the Shulammite's love for Solomon and why she loves him.

- ∾ What are the pitfalls and dangers of love based on physical beauty? How could this focus lead to jealousy and adultery?

- ∾ If this story is allegorical, the love may be spiritual. Is there such a thing as spiritual jealousy? Spiritual adultery? How do you know? Read James 4:4 and 2 Corinthians 11:2-3 to spark discussion.

- ∾ What can you apply to your physical and spiritual life?

THOUGHT FOR THE WEEK

The love between Solomon and the Shulammite was as beautiful as their own physical bodies. It was passionate, it was unique, and it was based on more than physical beauty. This woman had character. Solomon was attracted to her physical beauty, but he was also attracted to her character.

She worked hard in a vineyard for her mother and brothers. She turned brown from the sun—so much so that others stared at her. We also know that she was chaste—a wall that shut out all advances of men rather than a door that let them in. And when she grew up, she was a woman men respected.

It's important for us to understand the kind of love that sustains a marriage. It's not just physical beauty, which is only skin deep. It's about deeper, inward things, like character. People talk about "inner beauty" and mean the person you are, the values you hold, the part that doesn't change when skin browns, spots, or wrinkles; when hair grays, whitens, or falls out; and when the shape you had early in life deteriorates. When the songwriter wrote "Love Will Keep Us Together," surely he wasn't referring merely to love for the exterior package.

In his letter to the Ephesians, Paul commanded husbands to love their wives as Christ loved the church. This is sacrificial love, love that gives up selfish things to build up the other. The goal is for the husband to love his wife in such a way that she has "no spot or wrinkle or any such thing" and is holy and blameless. That's what Christ does for His bride, the church.

What about wives? In the same passage, Paul calls wives to be subject to their husbands as to the Lord. Because the larger context is imitating Christ, if a husband wants to imitate Christ, he must love his wife as Christ loved the church, giving Himself up for her. The church must be subject to the Lord, not in suppression or oppression, but as an act of love. Husband or wife, parent or child, slave or master, the example is self-sacrifice, devotion to the other person for his or her good.

If you're not yet married, what should your goal for love be? It should be passionate, yet based on respect. No, not with 60 wives and 80 concubines. That's not the model. The model is "one man, one woman." Seek that inner beauty so that together you can build a basis for love. It doesn't matter if it's your first marriage, or second, or whatever. If you're about to get married, base your marriage on God's principles.

What if you're married but your marriage has lost mutual respect? The best news is that God restores. God is the agent of restoration. If you and your spouse are committed to restoration, God is on your side. There is time and hope for a marriage that lasts, that withstands the storms of life, if you determine to love as Christ loved the church. If you commit to each other's spiritual good from this time forward, God will honor your commitment and fill you with new strength.

And if your marriage is picture-perfect? Congratulations! Thank God because it's His doing, not yours. There are no picture-perfect husbands or wives. We must all work on our marital relationships and learn to love our spouses day by day, just as we have to work on our relationship with the Lord. It's not something we can put on autopilot.

But every married person can say, "I am my beloved's, and he is mine."

Theme of Song of Solomon:

	SEGMENT DIVISIONS		
Author:			CHAPTER THEMES
			1
Date:			2
			3
Purpose:			4
Key Words:			5
			6
			7
			8

LAMENTATIONS

INTRODUCTION TO LAMENTATIONS

෬෬෬෬෬

(handwritten: Jeremiah 1-3)

(handwritten: 2 more then decide)

Israel had broken their covenant with God. They had worshipped other gods, chasing after them like a harlot. God sent prophet after prophet to chasten them for their sin and urge them to return to Him. He sent the Assyrians to take the northern tribes, collectively called Israel, captive into the nations around them. By 722 BC, only the southern kingdom, Judah, remained free. But in their freedom, the people of Judah worshipped idols too. They did not learn from Israel's dispersion. They clung to the false hope that God would not scatter them because of His holy city and house.

But their sin was even more abominable than that of the northern tribes. The kings, priests, and people brought idols into the temple itself. They defiled the temple that they clung to in false hope. They rejected the prophets God sent them, even conspiring to kill Jeremiah. Consequently their punishment was worse. God sent Babylon to punish Judah more harshly than Assyria punished Israel.

In the final siege, famine and pestilence accompanied the sword. The kings, priests, and people were taken captive to Babylon, and the temple and city of Jerusalem were destroyed.

Looking at the destroyed temple and city and the conditions of the people in captivity, an eyewitness wrote down his laments—Hebrew poetry of grief, mourning, and cries for relief. Tradition holds that this eyewitness was Jeremiah.

Today, every year, Jews read these laments on the day that commemorates the destruction of the temple, the ninth day of Av on their calendar—*Tisha B'Av* in Hebrew. They mourn the destruction of the temple and hope for its restoration.

Time for devoting of popularity, power or money. Devoting to something other than God. Put God first

LONELINESS

∾∾∾∾∾

Have you ever felt abandoned and alone? Did you cry over your feelings and lament your circumstances? If so, you can relate to Lamentations, a sad book. It's a book of poetry of mourning, weeping, and lamenting over what has happened.

∾∾∾
DAY ONE

The first three days of this week we'll look at the setting (historical context) of Lamentations so we can appreciate its message. One principle of good interpretation is to let context rule, and context is discovered by careful observation. Another good habit, founded on the presupposition that Scripture is its own best commentary, is to cross-reference other places in God's Word that shed light on a passage. In a study guide like this, we suggest references we think are best, although you may find many more.

Let's start by looking at the relationship God established with Israel in the covenant of the law. Deuteronomy is one of the five books of Moses that together were called the law, the Torah (instruction), or the Pentateuch (five books).

Read Deuteronomy 5:6-15. Number the commandments

in your Bible. These first four of the Ten Commandments also appear in Exodus 20. What do you learn about Israel's relationship to God?

What will God do to Israel if they disobey? Read the following verses:

Deuteronomy 28:41,45-57,62-67

Deuteronomy 29:22-28

Deuteronomy 30:1-5,15-20

In your notebook, list things the Israelites were commanded to do with respect to God and idols. Then briefly list consequences for obedience or disobedience. One or two words will do for each.

God spelled out clearly what He expected and what Israel could expect. All Israel had to do was obey the law. Would they obey? We'll find out tomorrow.

DAY TWO

Now let's look at some events from historical books in the Old Testament to see what happened.

Read 2 Kings 21 and 2 Chronicles 33. List in your notebook things the kings and the people did that violated the four commandments you read about yesterday.

Compare the consequences of Judah's actions with the warnings in Deuteronomy. List these in your notebook.

Remember, we're only giving you a few cross-references. If you studied all of Kings and Chronicles, you'd see that this was a pattern for both Israel and Judah.

DAY THREE

We saw what God commanded and how the people responded. There were a few bright spots (especially during David's and Solomon's lifetimes, before the kingdom divided, and later during the reigns of Josiah and Hezekiah in the southern kingdom), but what you read was typical. Now let's look at one of God's messengers to the southern kingdom, the prophet Jeremiah.

Read the following passages from Jeremiah:

> Jeremiah 2:26-28
>
> Jeremiah 3:6-10
>
> Jeremiah 15:1-9
>
> Jeremiah 21:5-10
>
> Jeremiah 52:1-16

In your notebook, summarize what happened to Judah and why.

DAY FOUR

With this background, let's dig into Lamentations. Today read Lamentations 1, marking *Jerusalem (Zion), affliction, comfort(ed),* and *sin* (including synonyms, like *transgressions*). Put these on your bookmark.

One effective poetic device is personification, which is attributing human characteristics to things. Jerusalem (or Zion) was the capital of Judah, the southern kingdom. Look where

(dye yellow?)

you marked *Jerusalem* and note the personification. What has happened to Jerusalem? What's afflicting her?

DAY FIVE

Read Lamentations 1 again and mark references to *God.* List everything you learned about God in this chapter in your notebook. Remember to ask the 5 W's and an H. The texts have the answers. What qualities (characteristics) of God do you see? What has He done and why?

Our relationship to God is based on His character. What do you see that applies to your relationship with Him (good or bad)? Think about these things and spend some time in prayer between now and your next day's study.

Remember, we're studying not only to gain knowledge but also to know God and His ways, to let His Word mold our relationship with Him.

DAY SIX

Three laments in Lamentations start with the word *how.* In fact, the Hebrew name for this book comes from the first word of Lamentations 1:1, *Ekhah,* which means "how."

What phrase starts with *how?* Now read Lamentations 2:1 and 4:1 to see the pattern.

How does the "how" phrase in 1:1 relate to the rest of the chapter? Why is Jerusalem lonely? Is her loneliness her fault? Why or why not?

How does Jerusalem express her feelings? When you feel rejected, how do you express your loneliness? Is it justified?

Finally, determine a theme for Lamentations 1 and record it on LAMENTATIONS AT A GLANCE on page 105.

DAY SEVEN

Store in your heart: Lamentations 1:1
Read and discuss: Lamentations 1

QUESTIONS FOR DISCUSSION OR INDIVIDUAL STUDY

ల Discuss your insights about Jerusalem. Include her condition, the reasons she is in it, her reaction to it, and how she expresses her feelings toward it.

ల Discuss similar situations in your life. What led up to these situations? How did you respond to them?

ల What did you learn about God (His character and ways)?

ల How does this chapter describe the relationship between Jerusalem and God?

ల What is your relationship with God? Compare your relationship to God with Jerusalem's. Are there similarities, differences, or both? Describe them.

THOUGHT FOR THE WEEK

Lamentations is one of the Bible's books of poetry. The Hebrew text contains acrostics using the Hebrew alphabet. These are hidden in translations, so we miss this aspect of the poetry in our English versions. But we don't miss other characteristics, like parallelism between verses and personification.

What do "Jerusalem is like a widow" and "her roads mourn" mean? When the author says Jerusalem sinned greatly, what does he mean? How does a city sin? Aren't the people of the city the ones who sin? Or is the city actually the people and not just the buildings? Figures of speech like this express ideas in less straightforward words. Poetry requires us to either reach beyond ordinary definitions to what the words represent or redefine the words themselves based on how they're used. We have to dig a little more deeply for meanings in poetic verse than we do in historical narratives.

Lamentations is an expression of grief and mourning. We read in Jeremiah that the city of Jerusalem was broken into, and the house of the Lord and city were burned. Jeremiah 52:12-13 says that the Babylonians came to Jerusalem and burned the house of the Lord, the king's house, and all the houses of Jerusalem on the tenth day of the fifth month of the nineteenth year of Nebuchadnezzar, king of Babylon. Second Kings 25:8-9 records the date as the seventh day of the fifth month. It's easy to imagine that the destruction didn't occur in one day, so the range probably covers events in the month of Av in 586 BC.

After the Jews' 70-year captivity, Cyrus, king of Persia, gave them permission to return to their land. They started rebuilding the temple in 536 BC, but when they finished, it wasn't as beautiful as Solomon's temple, which the Babylonians had destroyed. Just before the birth of Jesus, Herod the Great began an expansion of that temple to make it greater than Solomon's. But in AD 70, after a Jewish revolt against Roman rule, the Romans destroyed the rebuilt temple and city on the ninth day of the fifth month (Av).

During the 70-year captivity, the Jews fasted in the fifth month to mourn the destruction of the temple (Zechariah 7:3). After the Roman destruction of the temple in AD 70, they fasted on the ninth of Av to mourn or lament. This eventually became the date to mourn both destructions. Today, on *Tisha B'Av*, the ninth of Av, the Jews fast and read the book of Lamentations.

Jerusalem has no temple today. The city is inhabited by Muslims, Christians, and Jews, and the Muslims control the temple mount, where the temple once stood. The walls of the city and temple mount we see today were built in the 1500s by a Muslim ruler who used some of the stones from Herod's temple. Jews still mourn this. Until a new temple is built, Jews will mourn the destruction of the single most important article used in their worship.

Think about the most sacred structure in your country. Maybe it's a government building or palace, something that is tied to the history and culture of your country and that represents its people. Try to imagine how you and your countrymen would feel if someone totally destroyed it and kept you from rebuilding it—for 2000 years. How would you react?

Can you identify with the sadness of the Jews in 586 BC, AD 70, and even today?

It's easier and certainly more carnal to say, "They deserve it. They sinned!" But what about us? Haven't we all sinned? (Read 1 John 1:8 and Romans 3:23 if you don't think so.)

So what do we deserve? (Paul provides the answer in Romans 6:23.)

But what do we receive when we believe the gospel? (Again, Romans 6:23 gives us the answer.)

How much more beautiful it will be for believers to be lifted from mourning over the temple to rejoicing over their salvation. Jeremiah 3:16 says a day will come when the ark of the covenant will not be remembered or made again. The context is not that the Jews will have completely turned away from God but rather that the destruction of the temple and the loss of the ark will no longer be important to them. Israel will move beyond the earthly copies of heavenly realities into the presence of the living God.

Those in Christ today already possess this reality. One day, we will enjoy our full inheritance, and there will be no more mourning and no more tears (Revelation 21:4). We look for that day. Come, Lord Jesus!

(Collette)
Dick Kean

GREAT IS THY FAITHFULNESS

Chapter 2 & 3

∾∾∾∾∾

"'The LORD is my portion,' says my soul, 'Therefore I have hope in Him'" (Lamentations 3:24). We need hope when things aren't going well. It doesn't matter whether a situation is our fault or not, whether it's just or unjust. It's good to have hope in every circumstance. But where is hope found? It's found in the one true God, whose "lovingkindnesses indeed never cease, for His compassions never fail" (Lamentations 3:22).

DAY ONE

Read Lamentations 2 today, marking the key words from your bookmark. Also mark *anger (wrath),*[9] *destroy,*[10] and *little ones,*[11] and add them to the bookmark.

DAY TWO

List what you learned about God and Jerusalem in your notebook. Reflect on what you learned about God. Who is the "daughter of Jerusalem" (the "daughter of Zion")?

DAY THREE

What did you learn about "the little ones" in chapter 2? How does verse 20 strike you? Do you think cannibalism occurred?

Read Deuteronomy 28:49-57 again. (You read this last week.) Also read Jeremiah 19:3-9.

What horror! But what happens in a siege, when there is no more food and people are crazed with starvation? What constrains people from such things? What were these people lacking?

Make note of the "how" statement that begins Lamentations 2. Remember that this is a pattern for three of the chapters of Lamentations.

Determine a theme for Lamentations 2 and record it on LAMENTATIONS AT A GLANCE on page 105.

DAYS FOUR & FIVE

Read Lamentations 3 today, marking the key words on your bookmark. Mark *remember* and add it to your bookmark. This is a long chapter, so we're giving you two days to do this assignment.

DAY SIX

Now make a list in your notebook of all you learn about God from Lamentations 3.

Who is speaking in this chapter? Is it Jeremiah? Read Jeremiah 37:15-16 and 38:6.

Cisterns hewn from rock held rainwater collected during rainy seasons so people had water to use in dry seasons. Cisterns were also sometimes used for prisons whether they were dry or not. Sometimes a stone covered the opening.

Record a theme for Lamentations 3 on LAMENTATIONS AT A GLANCE on page 105.

DAY SEVEN

 Store in your heart: Lamentations 3:22-23
Read and discuss: Lamentations 2–3

QUESTIONS FOR DISCUSSION OR INDIVIDUAL STUDY

- ∾ Discuss what you learned about God in these chapters, especially His anger (wrath), affliction, compassion, lovingkindness, and comfort.

- ∾ What did you learn about Jerusalem?

- ∾ What did you learn about the speaker in chapter 3? (You can discuss the possibility that it was Jeremiah.)

- ∾ What did you learn about returning to the Lord?

- ∾ What can you apply from these chapters?

THOUGHT FOR THE WEEK

One of my favorite passages is Lamentations 3:22-23: "The LORD's lovingkindnesses indeed never cease, for His compassions never fail. They are new every morning; great is Your faithfulness." I am blessed to be able to assign these for memory verses this week. I remember learning them in the late 1970s or early '80s. A praise chorus based on these verses was very popular back then, and I always hear the melody when I read or recite these wonderful words.

It's good to have such words of comfort. Certainly Judah needed them, and Jeremiah did too. It's hard to watch God's judgment come on someone you love and not know that it is wrapped in lovingkindness, that compassion is part of His character, and that His faithfulness is great.

We can easily be angry at people who are overly harsh or who are unjust and cruel. But we make our evaluations through flawed lenses. God's love is more than we can understand. Certainly it's superior to our love. And His justice is superior too. In fact, God's justice makes man's justice look unjust.

Israel turned away from the one true God, who rescued them from slavery in Egypt, led them into a land of milk and honey, defeated their enemies before them, and provided rain for them. All this they rejected in favor of idols made from wood they cut from trees, wood they shaped with their hands and covered in silver and gold, dressed in purple, and fastened with nails so they wouldn't fall over. They bowed down to these things they made and worshipped them.

We can understand why God was angry. The Jews broke their promise not to make idols. We know that broken promises bring consequences. And if consequences are spelled out beforehand, it's reasonable for them to fall on those who break the promises. But weren't the consequences Israel suffered harsh, even cruel and unusual?

Let's consider consequences as deterrents. How effective are they if they aren't serious enough to make people want to avoid them? We don't want bad things to happen to us, so tough consequences make us think twice about doing things we've been told not to do. We like pleasurable experiences, but we consider whether our enjoyment is worth the risk of any negative consequences. (Well, *sometimes* we make that consideration. Clearly we also do things without thinking.)

So if God gives stern consequences for disobedience, sends reminders through His prophets, and patiently gives His people opportunities to obey and/or repent, what's wrong with the judgments (consequences) His people experience? They're fair and just. And because they're designed to cause right attitudes and behaviors, they're expressions of love. Read Hebrews 12:4-11.

We don't really like to be disciplined. We're much fonder of compassion. But God's faithfulness won't let us go on doing what's wrong. He loves us—His lovingkindnesses indeed never cease. As the text says, if He causes grief, He will later have compassion according to His lovingkindness (Lamentations 3:32). God works grief and compassion together according to His character and for our good.

This is good to remember every morning, so we'll have hope.

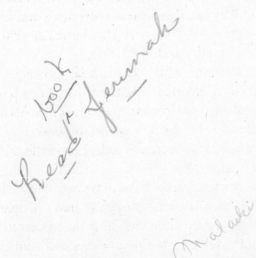

Regarded as Earthen Jars

God sent Jeremiah to the potter's house to show him that God is the potter and does whatever He wants with clay. If what He shapes is spoiled, He can reshape it. So can He reshape Israel. He also had Jeremiah break an earthen jar to show that He will break Israel. In Lamentations 4, God refers to "the precious sons of Zion, weighed against fine gold, how they are regarded as mere earthen jars." Contrasted to gold, they were something which, when broken, would be discarded as worthless.

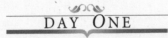

DAY ONE

Read Lamentations 4, marking the key words on your bookmark. Be sure to underline geographical references (things you could find on a map) in green. Also look for and note contrasts, like what someone *was* and *is now*.

DAY TWO

Read chapter 4 again. List the contrasts in your notebook and what you learned from each.

Famine and its consequences are mentioned again. Compare what you learn in this chapter with what you learned in the last lesson.

What did you learn about God's wrath in this chapter? If you made a list in your notebook from chapter 3, add to it.

DAY THREE

Lamentations 4:21-22 addresses Edom. Obadiah prophesied about 250 years before the events that Lamentations describes. Compare Obadiah 10-14 to Lamentations 4:21-22.

Obadiah may be referring to events that preceded the fall of Jerusalem, but we see interesting parallels, including Edom's attitude toward his nephew Judah (who descended from his brother Jacob, or Israel) and also God's judgment on Edom.

Record a theme for Lamentations 4 on LAMENTATIONS AT A GLANCE.

DAY FOUR

Read Lamentations 5, our final chapter, and mark key words. In this chapter, be sure to mark references to time.

DAY FIVE

What do you learn about God in chapter 5? What has happened in Zion and Judah? Is the situation different? What is different about this chapter—what distinguishes it from the other chapters?

Verse 7 says, "Our fathers sinned," but "we...have borne their iniquities." Is this fair? Read the following verses:

Exodus 20:4-5

Exodus 34:6-7

Numbers 14:18

Deuteronomy 5:9

DAY SIX

Read the following passages and then answer the questions that follow:

Jeremiah 25:11-12

Daniel 9:2-19

2 Chronicles 6:36-39

2 Corinthians 7:8-10

How long was the captivity to last? Forever? Was lamentation needed? What *was* needed?

Determine a theme for Lamentations 5 and record it on LAMENTATIONS AT A GLANCE.

Finally, consider the five chapter themes you've recorded on LAMENTATIONS AT A GLANCE and determine an overall theme for the book and record it on the chart too.

DAY SEVEN

 Store in your heart: Lamentations 5:19

Read and discuss: Lamentations 4–5

QUESTIONS FOR DISCUSSION OR INDIVIDUAL STUDY

∿ Review the circumstances of the people of Judah at the time of Lamentations. Then contrast them with circumstances in earlier days—what had things been like?

∿ Discuss Israel's reaction to their circumstances, including their understanding of why they were suffering. How did they see their future?

∿ Discuss the relationship between Edom and Judah.

∿ What lesson can we learn from Edom's future?

∿ What did you learn about God?

∿ What have you learned from this study of Lamentations that will impact your life? What truths will affect your relationship with God? What lessons about sorrow and repentance will you commit to live out?

THOUGHT FOR THE WEEK

Do you blame God when bad things happen to you? Or do you try to understand what He's teaching you? Your response to circumstances is critical, my friend, because your relationship to God is at stake. Do you trust God, or do you doubt Him? Do you bless or curse Him? Worship or ignore Him?

The Babylonians took most of the people of Judah captive. They took the treasures of the temple to Babylon, destroyed the temple and the city of Jerusalem, and killed their king and his sons. National identity was lost. The people of Judah were taken from the land God promised them, their worship system was destroyed, and their capital city was ruined. How would they react?

Lamentations records Judah's mourning over their destruction. The people knew their sin caused the destruction. They knew God poured out His wrath on them because of their sin. No excuses, no explanations, just an honest, "We sinned, and this happened because God judged justly."

How different this is from most people's reactions! Some shake their fist at God, saying, "It's all Your fault, and I hate You!" These people don't know God. God haters are not God's people. And blaming God is easy. It keeps you from having to take responsibility for your actions.

Others say, "Why me? What did I do?" These aren't God haters, but they too don't take responsibility. They argue their innocence, but at least they make the connection that actions have consequences. They just don't think they've done something bad enough to deserve what has happened.

Both groups will lament what happened. They'll mourn over their bad circumstances. But neither will take responsibility; neither will look inside to see if there was something they did to deserve judgment or if God is teaching them something.

Judah didn't react in either of these ways. Despite the people's grotesque idolatry and harlotry, Judah got the point. They finally saw their sin and confessed it. Jeremiah (or someone else writing under the Holy Spirit's inspiration) recorded this national lament in Lamentations.

The last few verses of the book reveal Judah's collective understanding of God—He rules. They know He rules forever, from generation to generation. But these verses also reveal that their understanding is incomplete. They know He rules forever, but they wonder why He forgets them forever.

If they had understood God's Word to them through Jeremiah, they would have known the captivity was set for 70 years. If they had understood God's Word to them through Isaiah, they would have known that their captivity would end when God raised up Cyrus to free them. They would have known their captivity would not last forever.

Calling on God to restore them acknowledged that God was the one who settled them in the land and then took them out of it. They acknowledged a national relationship with God but wondered if He had utterly rejected them.

Regardless of whether this lament was written immediately after the destruction of Jerusalem in 586 BC or closer to the end of their captivity in 539 BC, Judah's understanding of God was flawed. They did not understand God's message through the prophets. But the young prophet Daniel did. Daniel read Jeremiah's letter to the exiles, understood the length of the captivity, and realized that national repentance was needed. Lamentation is not repentance. Lamentation is sorrow over circumstances, not their moral causes. Repentance is sorrow for actions that caused the circumstances, seeing things the way God sees them, and then turning back to Him.

The Bible promises us trials. And we know trials are for the purpose of strengthening character. One important character trait is humility, which includes the ability to admit wrong, to confess sin. When bad things happen to you, how will you respond? Will you examine yourself to see if you need to repent of anything? Will you respond with worldly sorrow or with godly sorrow? What is your commitment to the Lord?

Will you praise God for circumstances that give you opportunities to draw closer to Him, to be shaped into more Christlike attitudes and behaviors? Remember, because you're in the New Covenant, you have a heart of flesh, not of stone, and you have God's Spirit in you to teach you, convict you, and empower you to obey His Word. You don't have to be like Judah, wondering if God has utterly rejected you. He hasn't! He's working in you to conform you into the likeness of His Son.

Theme of Lamentations:

SEGMENT DIVISIONS

		CHAPTER THEMES	Author:
		1	Date:
		2	Purpose:
			Key Words:
		3	
		4	
		5	

Notes

1. NIV: meaningless
2. KJV: vexation of spirit; NKJV: grasping for the wind; NIV: chasing after the wind
3. NIV, ESV: toil
4. KJV, NKJV, ESV: event
5. KJV, NKJV, ESV: vanity; NIV: meaningless
6. KJV, NKJV, NIV, ESV: find out, found out
7. KJV, NKJV, ESV: find out; NIV: comprehend
8. KJV, NKJV: fair; NIV: delightful
9. KJV, NKJV, ESV: fury
10. NIV: tear down
11. KJV, NKJV, NIV: children; ESV: infants, children

Books in the
New Inductive Study Series

∿∿∿∿

NEW AMERICAN STANDARD BIBLE
UPDATED EDITION

THE NEW INDUCTIVE STUDY BIBLE

DISCOVERING THE TRUTH FOR YOURSELF

CHANGING THE WAY PEOPLE STUDY GOD'S WORD

"Inductive study of the Bible is the best way to discover scriptural truth...There is no jewel more precious than that which you have mined yourself."

—HOWARD HENDRICKS

Every feature is designed to help you gain a more intimate understanding of God and His Word. This study Bible, the only one based entirely on the inductive study approach, provides you with the tools for observing what the text says, interpreting what it means, and applying it to your life.